2014

To Pam

Hope you
enjoy Michael's
book on Prayer

Love,
Sue

D0344883

THE POWER OF AN ORDINARY PRAYER

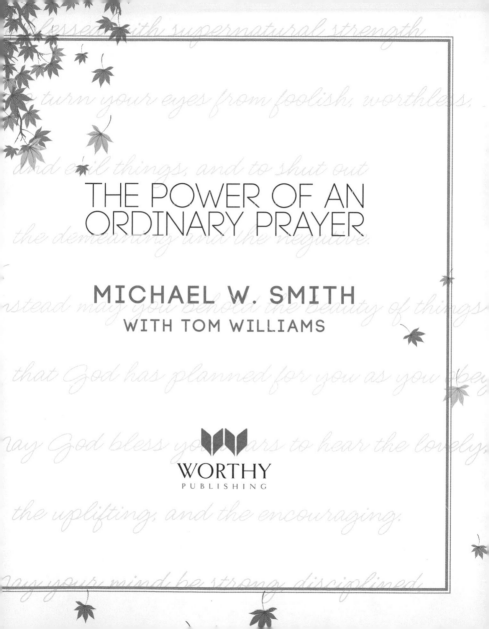

THE POWER OF AN ORDINARY PRAYER

MICHAEL W. SMITH
WITH TOM WILLIAMS

WORTHY
PUBLISHING

Copyright © 2013 by Michael W. Smith

ISBN 978-1-617-95192-3

Published by Worthy Publishing, a division of Worthy Media, Inc., 134 Franklin, Road, Suite 200, Brentwood, Tennessee 37027.

HELPING PEOPLE EXPERIENCE THE HEART OF GOD

Library of Congress Control Number: 2013939292

Published in association with Chaz Corzine and Greg Ham, The MWS Group, Franklin, Tennessee.

Cover design: Koechel Peterson and Associates

Interior design: ThinkpenDesign.com

Printed in the United States of America

13 14 15 16 17 18   LBM   9 8 7 6 5 4 3 2 1

DEDICATION

Among the many blessings of my life was Debbie's grandmother, Kate Washburn—"Nanny" to the kids and "Kate Dear" to me! I never felt like an in-law; she welcomed me into the family, as her own grandson, from the very start. Of her ninety-six years, I was privileged to know her for more than twenty-nine years—years that she filled with love of family, compassion for others, and commitment to the Lord. Oh, and her one-liners were legendary! No one was around Kate for long without getting a taste of her humor! So I lovingly dedicate this book to Nanny. I look forward to the tremendous blessing of being with her again, forever this time.

CONTENTS

BLESSED TO BE A BLESSING

I have been blessed all my life. I'm not speaking just of the abundance of what God has given me, though those blessings are extravagant and too many to count. I mean I have been blessed verbally all my life. Godly people have actually said words of blessing to me. As far back as I can remember, my dad and mom have blessed me. Not only by being amazing, loving, and supportive parents, though they were every inch that. They blessed me with words. With encouragement. With positive reinforcement. There's no way to calculate how much good that did me in my growing-up years. There's no doubt that I am the man I am today because of my mom and dad.

Later, Don Finto, who was pastor of the Belmont Church in Nashville, became a greatly respected mentor to me. He often spoke a blessing over me—and he still does to this day.

These spoken blessings have been such a big part of my life that I guess it was natural for me to say blessings over others. I still do it. For example, when a member of my band was leaving rehearsal to embark on a trip, I sent him on his way with a blessing.

Fairly recently, this idea of praying blessings over people has gained an even larger importance for me. Let me tell you why.

Just so there won't be any misunderstanding, let me say emphatically, right here and now, that there is nothing "magical" about this prayer of blessing. In fact, it's rather ordinary. It's not a formula to assure you of vast material blessings or even of a trouble-free Christian life. It's nothing like an incantation or a discovery of some secret buried deep in an obscure Old Testament passage that will mystically turn your life around. It is not something you can use to manipulate God into giving you whatever you want. God does not respond to words or formulas. He responds to the heart. There is no way we can use prayer or God's promise of blessing to gain what we term today as "the good life." God's real blessings are not of that sort. They are better.

Yet I am convinced that in this book you will find simple, biblical principles of living that can turn your spiritual life into something beautiful that soars above the mundane and finds the true joy that God yearns for each of us to experience. That is the blessing I pray that you will find as you read this book.

This book breaks the prayer I pray into its six specific blessings. Each chapter begins with a quote containing the segment of the blessing it will address. Then the chapter explains the value of the blessing and gives practical guidance in how to open oneself to the blessing and enjoy its benefits.

Let me remind you, as you read, that you are the son or daughter of the King. Not *a* king, but *the* King—the King of the universe. As his child, you are the heir to all he has. My fear is that we, like the prodigal son in Jesus' parable, can miss out on this enormous blessing awaiting us in trust by grasping for the immediate gratification of wealth, pleasure, comfort, and entertainment offered by the culture around us. That is the tragedy I fear may be happening to many Christians today. And that is the tragedy that can be averted if we understand the true nature of God's real blessings.

I am convinced that if you humble yourself before our Father, submit to him and his will for your life, and pray earnestly that he will bless you, you can receive an extraordinary blessing far beyond what you can imagine.

That is the blessing I pray that you will find in this book.

THE PRAYER OF BLESSING

In the name of Jesus Christ,
I bless you with the promises of God,
which are "yes" and "amen."

May the Holy Spirit make you healthy
and strong in body, mind, and spirit
to move in faith and expectancy.
May God's angels be with you to
protect and keep you.

Be blessed with supernatural strength
to turn your eyes from
foolish, worthless, and evil things, and to shut out
the demeaning and the negative.

Instead may you behold the beauty of things
that God has planned for you
as you obey his Word.
May God bless your ears to hear the lovely,
the uplifting, and the encouraging.
May your mind be strong, disciplined,
balanced, and faith-filled.

May your feet walk in holiness and
your steps be ordered by the Lord.
May your hands be tender and helping,
blessing those in need.
May your heart be humble and
receptive to one another
and to the things of God, not to the world.

God's grace be upon your home,
that it may be a sanctuary of rest and renewal,
a haven of peace where sounds of joy
and laughter grace its walls,
where love and unconditional acceptance
of one another is the constant rule.

May God give you the spiritual strength to
overcome the evil one
and avoid temptation.
May God's grace be upon you to
fulfill your dreams and visions.
May goodness and mercy follow you
all the days of your long life.

CHAPTER 1

PRAYING FOR . . .
THE PROMISES OF GOD

*In the name of Jesus Christ, I bless you with the
promises of God, which are "yes" and "amen."*

For all of God's promises have been fulfilled in
Christ with a resounding "Yes!" And through Christ,
our "Amen" . . . ascends to God for his glory.

2 CORINTHIANS 1:20 NLT

*S*ome believers are missing out on God's promises because they misunderstand what his real blessings are about. They don't feel blessed, because they are looking for a thorn-free rose garden blooming with all the stuff that will make their lives comfortable, prosperous, and pain-free.

Let me repeat here what I said in the introduction. The prayer I pray will not bring this kind of blessing. There is nothing magical about this prayer. It's not a formula to assure you of an abundant life or an incantation designed to manipulate God into giving you whatever you want. In fact, it's rather ordinary—but it contains extraordinary power to bring God's blessings into your life.

God never promised us a rose garden. At least, not in this life. He did give us a perfect garden once, and we—that is, our distant grandparents Adam and Eve—messed it up. Now we must live with that mess. But God promises that if we will deal with that mess in his way and, by his grace, contend with the weeds and thorns and rust and rot, he will bless us. Not necessarily by taking all the problems away, but by shaping us into his image as we press through those problems. Even as we walk through the greatest hardships of life, we have the assurance that God will eventually lead us to that new and perfect garden we long for after we finish our term here. Jesus himself made the promise: "I go to prepare a place for you. If I go and prepare a place for you, I will come again and receive you to Myself, that where I am, there you may be also" (John 14:2–3 NASB).

This promise of perfection in the future does not mean God has no blessings for us here and now. Not by a long shot! In fact, God promises that if we uphold his truth and walk in his ways, he will give us not only that new garden in the future, but also real joy in this life now (John 10:10). What we need to learn, however, is that joy is not dependent on getting every desire met—that is, not those desires that infect us from the virus of today's me-culture.

Real joy comes when we get the right desire met—the desire for God himself, for a life led by the Spirit, fulfilling not our material desires but our deepest need, which is to be in a close relationship with our Creator. That is the source of true blessing. The only source.

If my ordinary prayer of blessing awakens people to this true source of real and extraordinary blessings, I am deeply gratified. I hope that, once awakened, people will not fall asleep again but rather take positive steps to change their approach to their journey of faith. To stop pursuing a self-oriented lifestyle. To become unselfish. To address the needs of others. I hope my prayer of blessing will inspire them to pray a similar blessing upon others.

BECOMING AN INSTRUMENT FOR BLESSING

*W*hen people pray for blessings, I hope they will then take one more step. I hope they will become actively involved in being instruments in God's hands to bring the blessings they pray for into the lives of the people they know—family, friends, coworkers.

GOD BLESSED ABRAHAM TO BE A BLESSING TO OTHERS
(GENESIS 12:2). IN WHAT WAYS HAVE GOD'S PROMISES
BLESSED YOUR LIFE? HOW HAVE THEY LED YOU TO
BLESS OTHERS?

*W*hat does it mean to be an instrument in God's hands? Let me illustrate: I have a piano in my living room. It's one of my favorite instruments. When I'm writing a new song, I'll sit at that piano. I may jot down a few chord changes of the song on a scratch pad, adding notes and revising the melody until I think I have something worth pursuing. Then I will refine and polish the song until it's ready to play. But that song remains an inaudible thought in my head or on paper until I play it on my piano. In other words, nothing is heard until my fingers hit the keys and the hammers hit the strings. My piano turns my thoughts and emotions into sounds. These sounds flow out of the piano as music to the ears of listeners and, I hope, into their hearts. In other words, the piano incarnates my intent into something tangible that can affect others.

Jesus understood this principle. He was God the Father's instrument to convey his invisible mind and heart to his creation. Over and over in John's gospel, Jesus repeated that in everything he said or did, he was just passing on the heart and mind of God. He passed on to others what God the Father gave to him. He was the instrument, the conveyer of the blessing (John 5:19; 12:49–50; 14:10, 24, 31).

We are to bless others as Jesus did. We don't originate the blessing; God originates it, and it resounds through us just as my music resounds through the piano in my living room. Just as God's love resounded through the life of Jesus.

The importance of being God's instrument hits home with full force when we realize that when Jesus ascended to heaven, he took his body with him. This means God no longer has a body on earth through which he can bless others—except ours. We are charged with the task of being the body of Jesus in the world today. As Paul said, "Now you are the body of Christ, and each one of you is a part of it" (1 Cor. 12:27). We are to take up where Jesus left off. He now depends on us to take up the task Jesus was performing and convey God's heart and mind to others. To take the blessings God gives us and bless others with them.

Okay, I know this is not exactly an original idea. We've been singing songs about being "channels of blessing" for generations. I've written some myself over the course of my career. Songs like "Live the Life," "Give It Away," and "Open Arms" deal with the theme of being the hands and feet of Jesus to the world.

The idea of being God's instrument to bless others may not be new, but it is still valid—more than valid; it's vital. And I'm including it here because it is the only effective antidote to today's me-culture. The e-mails I receive, as well as what I see in the lives of people of faith, strongly indicate that this is true.

A LIFE OF SELFLESS GIVING

I've been blessed with the opportunity to travel the world to lead in corporate worship people from almost every culture you can imagine. Within these opportunities, there were specific moments when the sense of God's presence was so real, and the people's response so genuine, that it was too much for me to handle. After moments like these I often find myself facedown on my dressing room floor. But just as often, I find myself asking nagging questions like, "Was that as real for everybody else as it was for me?" Or, "Is what we experienced out there going to spur anyone on to developing the Spirit of Christ in their hearts, or was it just an emotional experience that made people feel better about themselves?" I am very aware that people can be involved in the Christian life purely for the mountaintop experiences.

WHEN WAS THE LAST "MOUNTAINTOP" EXPERIENCE YOU HAD WITH GOD? HOW DID YOU FEEL ABOUT THE EXPERIENCE? WAS THERE ANY LASTING CHANGE AS A RESULT OF THIS EXPERIENCE?

*T*his stands in stark contrast to people I have met who have allowed the reality of what God has done for them to so overtake them that they have dedicated their lives to the service of others. I came across them all the time while serving on the President's Council on Service and Civic Participation. If you were to write a story about these people's lives, the main plot would not be about them but about the people around them. These are people who know what it means to be an instrument.

When it comes to understanding what it means to be God's instrument, I love the prayer of Saint Francis of Assisi. I can't think of a better way to end this chapter than with his thoughts:

Lord, make me an instrument of your peace.

Where there is hatred, let me sow love;

where there is injury, pardon;

where there is doubt, faith;

where there is despair, hope;

where there is darkness, light;

where there is sadness, joy.

O Divine Master,

grant that I may not so much seek to be consoled as
   to console;

to be understood, as to understand;

to be loved, as to love;

for it is in giving that we receive,

it is in pardoning that we are pardoned,

and it is in dying that we are born to eternal life.

Amen.

In this selfless kind of giving to others, Saint Francis discovered the key to God's true blessings. Far from being a way to achieve success, ease, and comfort, Christianity calls us to live a life that forgets self and focuses on being God's instrument to show his love to others.

That is what I am learning from this simple prayer of blessing. And that is what I want to convey to you in the chapters that follow.

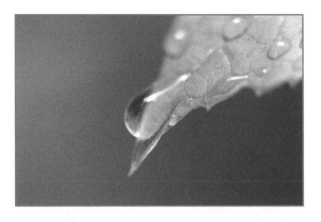

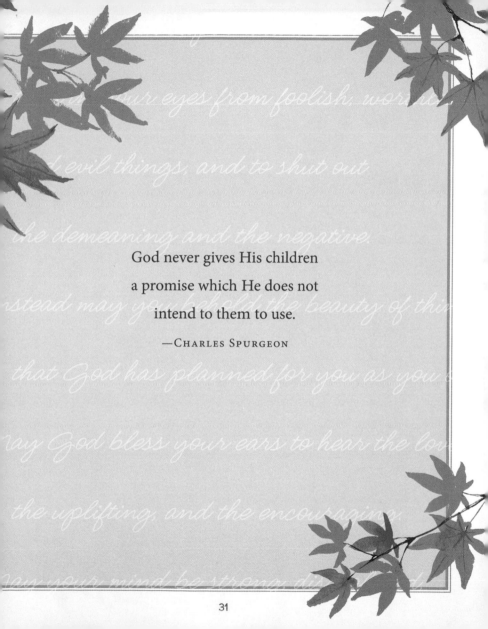

God never gives His children
a promise which He does not
intend to them to use.

—CHARLES SPURGEON

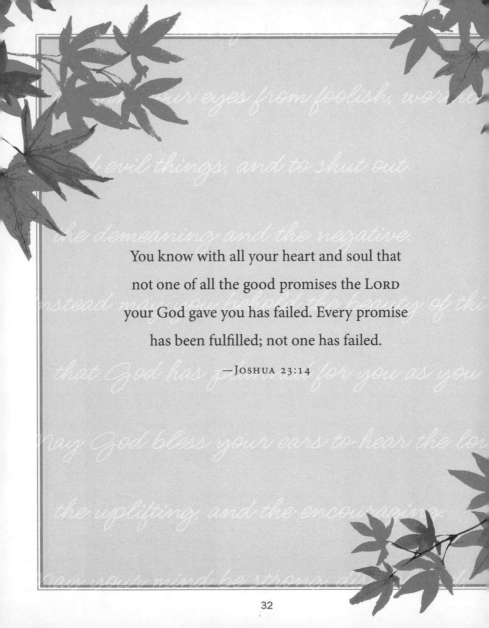

You know with all your heart and soul that
not one of all the good promises the Lord
your God gave you has failed. Every promise
has been fulfilled; not one has failed.

—Joshua 23:14

FOR REFLECTION AND ACTION

HOW CAN YOU TAKE THE PROMISES OF GOD AND BE
AN INSTRUMENT IN HIS HANDS TODAY? OVER THE NEXT
WEEK? OVER THE NEXT YEAR?

CHAPTER 2

PRAYING FOR . . . SPIRITUAL HEALTH

May the Holy Spirit make you healthy and strong in
body, mind, and spirit to move in faith and expectancy.
May God's angels be with you to protect and keep you.

Dear friend, I pray that you may enjoy good
health and that all may go well with you,
even as your soul is getting along well.

—3 JOHN 2

*W*hen God placed Adam and Eve in the Garden of Eden, he "blessed them" (Gen. 1:28). What does that mean? Well, when you look at the setup they had, it's obvious, isn't it? God gave this first couple everything they could think to ask for—and more. I'm not exaggerating when I say that no one ever had it so good. Adam and Eve are the only people ever to live on this planet who experienced absolute perfection in every way possible.

Adam and Eve themselves were perfect. Adam reflected God's design of the ideal man, and Eve was his flawless counterpart. Their relationship was perfect. They never had a spat, never got their feelings hurt, never pouted. Their love life was idyllic and fulfilling. Adam was always thoughtful, loving, and romantic, and Eve never had a headache. They never got sick, never aged. Their daily menu consisted of the most delicious foods, abundantly available simply for the taking. The climate and weather were so perfect they didn't bother to wear clothing, yet they never punctured a foot on a grass burr or scratched their skin on a thorn because burrs and thorns did not exist. They had an open-ended lease on a grand estate filled with towering trees, lush green grass, clear springs, and flowing rivers. No doubt about it, Adam and Eve had it made. They were enormously blessed.

But hold everything. When we read a little more about that Genesis blessing, we find that there were responsibilities attached: "Then God blessed them and said, 'Be fruitful and multiply. Fill the earth and govern it" (Gen. 1:28 NLT). So they were not just passive recipients of blessing; there was something Adam and Eve had to do in order to experience God's blessing. They were charged to multiply and govern.

Well now, are those tough conditions or what! Most people are eager to engage in that "be fruitful and multiply" process even without being urged. And the idea of ruling seems to appeal to just about everyone. We like to be in control, whether it's as the CEO of a big corporation or just having a space to call our own. But if all we see in these requirements attached to God's blessing is more gratification of natural desires, we may be missing their deeper meaning.

While the initial process of being fruitful and multiplying is no chore, the result of it certainly is. Raising kids brings huge responsibilities and requires painful sacrifices. And the idea of governing the earth or at least being king of some little hill appeals to our natural instincts—until we remember Jesus telling his disciples, "Whoever wants to be a leader among you must be your servant, and whoever wants to be first among you must become your slave" (Matt. 20:26–27 NLT). That dulls the glitter just a little, doesn't it?

THE BLESSING THAT BLESSES OTHERS

$\mathcal{G}$od's blessings involve more than just passive receiving. With every blessing that has a benefit for us, there seems to be a corresponding responsibility to others. We have a natural tendency to love the "me" part and to pretty much forget about the "others" part.

That's our big problem. The two parts of blessing are wrapped up in one package. The blessing received is not complete until we meet the requirement attached to it. And it seems that the requirement always involves a responsibility to others. The blessing blesses us not just by flowing from God into our lives, but by flowing on out of our lives to others.

As we discussed in the previous chapter, the piano in my living room doesn't take the music I put into it and bottle it up inside, cherish it, and consider it a private matter between itself and me. It doesn't get emotional and go into a religious ecstasy when I'm playing it and figure that's the end purpose of its being. The blessing is not complete until it passes through the instrument (there's that word again) and becomes music to the people who hear it. A blessing kept to one's self is no blessing at all.

Can you imagine Jesus leaving the glory of the throne room of heaven to come to earth only to run off to a mountaintop to spend his days communing privately with God in prayer and scroll reading? Can you imagine the apostle Paul after his dramatic conversion becoming a pious churchgoer, listening to the choir and sermons and then expecting God to bless him for having those tingling religious feelings by expanding his tent-making business into a multinational corporation?

No. Paul knew the drill. His attitude was not, "Now that I've had this encounter with Christ, I expect God to pour his blessings into me." It was, "Lord, open me up to pass on your blessings to others." And did Paul ever bless others! He undoubtedly wins the award as the most successful evangelist ever; through his missionary journeys and biblical writings, he spread the good news of Jesus to more people than any one person has ever reached since.

IT IS EASY TO DESIRE THE BENEFITS OF SPIRITUAL HEALTH AND PROSPERITY WITHOUT THE HARD WORK AND SACRIFICE. IN WHAT WAYS MAY YOU HAVE TRIED TO DO THIS IN YOUR OWN LIFE? WHAT WERE YOUR EXPECTATIONS? WHAT ARE YOUR EXPECTATIONS NOW?

So, what kind of life did Paul have as a result of his significant work for God? Paul gave us the answer in his own words:

"Five times I received from the Jews the forty lashes minus one. Three times I was beaten with rods, once I was stoned, three times I was shipwrecked, I spent a night and a day in the open sea, I have been constantly on the move. I have been in danger from rivers, in danger from bandits, in danger from my own countrymen, in danger from Gentiles; in danger in the city, in danger in the country, in danger at sea; and in danger from false brothers. I have labored and toiled and have often gone without sleep; I have known hunger and thirst and have often gone without food; I have been cold and naked" (2 Cor. 11:24–27).

I can guess what you're thinking, because it's hard for me not to think it myself: *Wow! If this is what you call blessing, I don't want any part of it.* But before we engrave that thought in our hearts, let's delve a little deeper into Paul's life. True, he seems to have had more than his share of hard knocks. Yet to read his letters, you'd think he was the happiest man who ever lived. He loved the words *joy*, *joyful*, and *rejoice*, using them repeatedly in his letters, often with great enthusiasm, as in this passage: "Rejoice in the Lord always. I will say it again: Rejoice!" (Phil. 4:4). In every instance he was speaking of his own joy or the joy of being in Christ that he shares with other Christians.

It pains me to say it, but there's no doubt that many Christians today have turned that idea on its head. Often the authenticity of the Christian life is judged by how richly one has been blessed with the things that make up what we call "the good life"—a nice house, new cars, a successful career, and a bulging bank account. When we see a Christian possessing all this stuff, we're likely to think, *God has really blessed him, so he must be doing something right.*

Don't get me wrong: some authentic Christians who are living truly godly lives do have this kind of material success. It's not a sin to be wealthy. God knows who can handle wealth and use it well and who cannot, and I believe it's likely that he gives or withholds accordingly. The point I'm making is that these material blessings, though God may choose to give them, are not the true measure of one's spiritual health.

The call of Christ was never an invitation to a materially abundant, trouble-free life of comfort and achievement. No, it is and always has been a call to die. Jesus himself said this about as clearly as it could be said:

> If any of you wants to be my follower, you must turn from your selfish ways, take up your cross, and

follow me. If you try to hang on to your life, you will lose it. But if you give up your life for my sake, you will save it. And what do you benefit if you gain the whole world but lose your own soul? Is anything worth more than your soul? (Matt. 16:24–26 NLT)

"Take up your cross," Jesus says. What does that mean? We see Christian crosses everywhere. On top of church steeples and hanging in church sanctuaries, on gravesites, book covers, bumper stickers, and posters; we decorate them and wear them as jewelry. We're so used to the cross as the symbol of Christianity that we no longer think about its original purpose as an instrument designed to inflict suffering and death.

WHAT DOES "TAKING UP THE CROSS OF CHRIST" MEAN TO YOU? HOW DOES THIS RELATE TO THE IDEA OF SPIRITUAL HEALTH?

....

....

....

....

....

....

....

....

....

....

....

....

But when Jesus told us to take up our cross, he *was* thinking of its original purpose. He meant we must die to ourselves—we must consider ourselves dead to the self-oriented instinct that makes us cling to our own ambitions, pleasures, and comfort. That means giving your life to Christ and being consistently guided by his Spirit. If this puts you in a situation where you must suffer, well, join the club. Its members include Paul, the apostles, Christ himself, and millions of Christians who have suffered since.

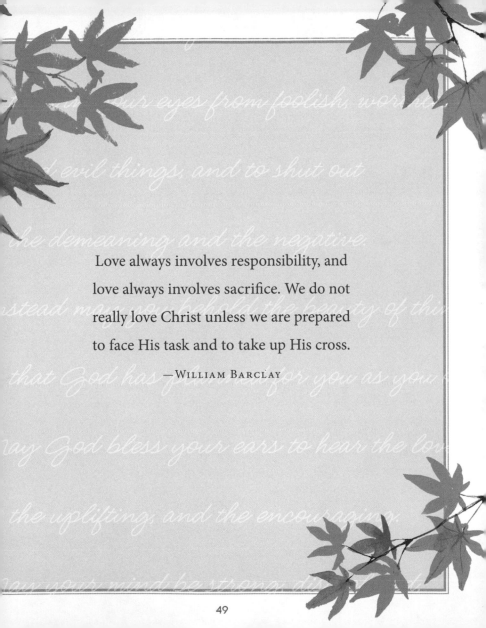

Love always involves responsibility, and
love always involves sacrifice. We do not
really love Christ unless we are prepared
to face His task and to take up His cross.

—William Barclay

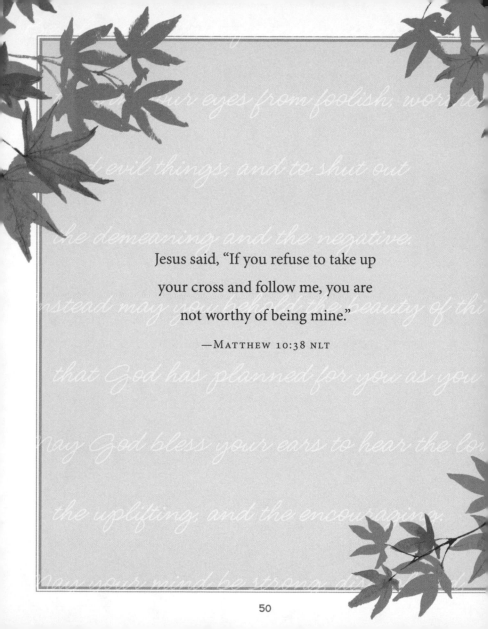

Jesus said, "If you refuse to take up
your cross and follow me, you are
not worthy of being mine."

—Matthew 10:38 nlt

FOR REFLECTION AND ACTION

DYING TO SELF AND LIVING FOR JESUS BRINGS ENORMOUS BLESSINGS: PEACE, JOY, LOVE, AND GRACE. HOW, SPECIFICALLY, CAN YOU TAKE UP YOUR CROSS TODAY IN ORDER TO BE A BLESSING TO OTHERS?

CHAPTER 3

PRAYING FOR . . . A PURE MIND

Be blessed with supernatural strength to turn your eyes from
foolish, worthless, and evil things, and to shut out the demeaning
and the negative. Instead may you behold the beauty of things that
God has planned for you as you obey his Word. May God bless
your ears to hear the lovely, the uplifting, and the encouraging.
May your mind be strong, disciplined, balanced, and faith-filled.

Friends, I'd say you'll do best by filling your minds and meditating
on things true, noble, reputable, authentic, compelling, gracious—
the best, not the worst; the beautiful, not the ugly; things to praise,
not things to curse. . . . Do that, and God, who makes everything
work together, will work you into his most excellent harmonies.

—Philippians 4:8 msg

$\mathcal{M}$y reason for concern about what we absorb into our minds is simple. You've heard it said, "You are what you eat." We become what we fill ourselves with. The computer savvy say it like this: "Garbage in, garbage out." Fill your mind with violent images, and you're more likely to become violent. Fill it with sexual images, and you're likely to become lustful. Fill it with images of compromise, acceptance of cultural practices and values, and you're likely to adopt those values as your own. Fill it with inanity and you lose the discernment to become all God intended you to be.

Even if we believers don't adopt the culture's values overtly, we have a perverse capacity to adapt these values to our own wants. I've heard Christians say they fudge on their income taxes, but they feel justified because they don't approve of how the government wastes their money and promotes immoralities such as abortion or bans on prayer.

Some Christians justify cutting corners in their businesses because it enables them to give more money to the church.

I have even heard of one executive in a faith-based company who deliberately delayed payment to suppliers because the extra interest he earned by holding the money longer was "good stewardship of God's resources." It doesn't take much imagination to wonder what this man's vendors thought of his character.

These sad facts show that it's not realistic to think we can fill our minds with corrupting images yet hang on to what we know is right. When we continually expose our minds to the standards of the culture, those standards begin to seep into our lives. The fatal change comes so gradually that, like the frog in the kettle, we don't even notice it. First we are no longer shocked by evil. Then we become accustomed to it. Then we tolerate it. Then it's only a tiny step to accept it as normal.

AVOIDING CULTURAL CONTAMINATION

To receive God's blessing and become blessers ourselves, Paul urged us to "stay away from every kind of evil" (1 Thess. 5:22 NLT). That means we must avoid the contamination of the surrounding culture. Easier said than done, Paul. How can we avoid exposure to the evils of our culture? Should we pull up stakes and move into an isolated commune with other believers or find an uninhabited island somewhere? No, Paul recognized that we must interact with all kinds of people, good and evil (1 Cor. 5:9–11). He means we must find a way to keep those evil influences from ruining our character.

So how do we keep the surrounding cultural contamination from filling our minds? Paul's answer: "Don't copy the behavior and customs of this world, but let God transform you into a new person by changing the way you think. Then you will learn to know God's will for you, which is good and pleasing and perfect" (Rom. 12:2 NLT).

I would love to change the way I think so I am open to God's will. But how do I do that? The culture is all around me. Every TV show has some kind of immorality. If it doesn't, the commercials do. It's everywhere I look— billboards, movies, ads in the mall, business practices. How do I avoid its influence?

Again, Paul has the answer: "Fix your thoughts on what is true, and honorable, and right, and pure, and lovely, and admirable. Think about things that are excellent and worthy of praise" (Phil. 4:8 NLT). There's nothing mysterious about that; it's just plain and simple logic. You don't want your mind filled with contamination? Well, then, fill it with something pure. (Do we sometimes make this more complex than it really is, or what?) To fill your mind with cultural garbage leaves no room for God to pour in the blessings he wants you to enjoy.

HOW DOES WHAT A PERSON THINKS ABOUT AFFECT THE WAY THEY LIVE THEIR LIFE? WHAT ABOUT THE THINGS A PERSON ALLOWS INTO THEIR MIND THROUGH MOVIES, MUSIC, TELEVISION, ETC.? DOES IT HAVE AN IMPACT ON THEIR SPIRITUAL HEALTH? IF SO, WHAT INFLUENCE DOES IT HAVE?

SETTING OUR EYES ON THE POSITIVE

$\mathcal{T}$his need to fill our minds with things that are "excellent and worthy" is what prompted me to add the next phrase in my blessing: "May you behold the beauty of things that God has planned for you as you obey his Word. May God bless your ears to hear the lovely, the uplifting, and the encouraging."

Even though the corruption of culture surrounds us like polluted air, it is always possible to find the good that remains inherent in God's creation. We can do this because as believers we have the privilege of calling on the power of the Holy Spirit within us to resist those evil influences and hold instead to God's standard of good. Even though our sinful natures may undermine our attempts to meet that standard, we can stand strong.

WHAT ARE THE QUALITIES OF WHOLESOME THOUGHTS (SEE PHILIPPIANS 4:8)? WHAT WOULD IT TAKE TO THINK PURE THOUGHTS IN OUR CULTURE TODAY?

....

....

....

....

....

....

....

....

....

....

....

....

....

We have the assurance that God's grace is sufficient for us, freeing us from the bondage of legalism. We are no longer locked up by a sense of duty; instead, we are compelled to holy living by his great love for us. Because of this grace, we are free to live our lives in a way that reflects his purity. We can refuse to lower the bar in order to justify our failure. We will never grow into the glorious creatures God knows we can be unless we keep his high standard as our goal, not the standards culture sets for what is righteous and what isn't. We can increase our capacity for obedience to God's leading by keeping our eyes and ears attuned to what is good, lovely, uplifting, encouraging, and positive.

God created us in his own image. Of course, that doesn't mean we can be God as he is; it means we can become little duplicates of him. We won't achieve the glorious potential God has in store for us if we keep our eyes lowered to the mirror of merely what is; we must lift them to the window of what can be. That's why the antiheroes of today's entertainment can hurt us. They keep us glued to the mirror instead of the window. If we want to do more than just drift along in the cultural stream, it helps to search out models of goodness, purity, honor, character, and courage, both in our entertainment and in real life.

Why are such models helpful? Because sometimes the desire for greatness incubates better in the imagination than in the will. An inspiring example motivates us better than a sermon. Mustering up the will to reach higher seems like a lot of hard work. It means waging a serious battle with that sin nature that's sure to snarl and fight back at any attempt to muzzle it. But watching a Maximus in *Gladiator* or an Oskar Schindler in *Schindler's List* or a William Wallace in *Braveheart* kindles our better instincts and makes us long to be grander than we are. These heroes open a window and let in a refreshing blast of clean air that inspires us with a glimpse of what we can be. The great advantage to having such heroes is that they don't badger us into changing; they inspire us to want to change.

God created the world pure and uncontaminated. Our original ancestors misused it, and the result is the rust of death, pain, grief, and all the troubles we deal with now. But God values his creation, and he fully intends to remove the rust and restore everything to its original uncontaminated perfection.

That is the ultimate reality. That is true realism. The ugly stuff we contend with day by day is the rust. The stuff we see portrayed in TV and films and other forms of entertainment mistakenly treats the rust as the reality. So when we choose to set our eyes and ears on purer things, when we learn to prefer real heroes and happy endings, we are showing our commitment to the true reality that God has promised. The story God wrote has a happy-ever-after ending that promises eternal joy to those who focus on the pure and lovely and adopt true character into their lives. If we focus our eyes and ears on things that give us glimpses of that happy reality, it will go a long way toward enabling us to receive the blessings God wants to pour into us.

That is why I pray so fervently that you and I will commit ourselves to turning away from the foolish, worthless, evil, demeaning, and negative things the culture thrusts at us. I pray that we will focus instead on the lovely, the uplifting, and the encouraging. That's where we find true blessing. And that's how we can become blessings to others who need models to show them the truth they so desperately need to know.

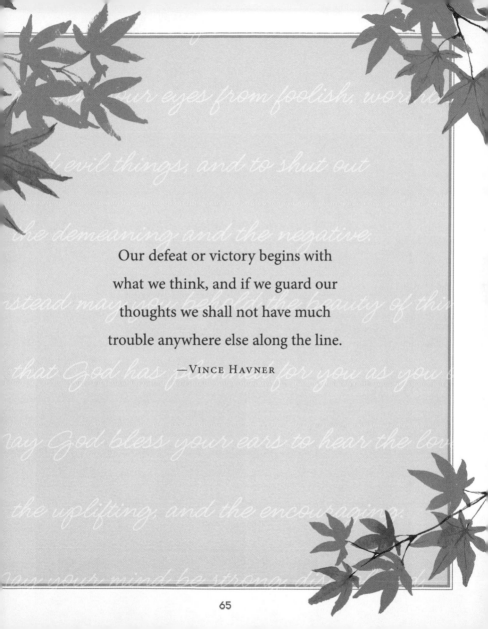

Our defeat or victory begins with
what we think, and if we guard our
thoughts we shall not have much
trouble anywhere else along the line.

—VINCE HAVNER

FOR REFLECTION AND ACTION

HOW CAN YOU, IN THE NEXT WEEK, BEGIN TO PURIFY YOUR MIND AND FOCUS MORE ON THE THINGS OF GOD? WHAT TV SHOWS, MOVIES, OR MUSIC MIGHT YOU NEED TO ELIMINATE? WHAT THINGS MIGHT YOU NEED TO ADD TO YOUR SPIRITUAL DISCIPLINES?

As he thinketh in his heart, so is he.

—Proverbs 23:7 KJV

CHAPTER 4

PRAYING FOR . . .
PERSONAL HOLINESS

May your feet walk in holiness and your steps be ordered by
the Lord. May your hands be tender and helping, blessing
those in need. May your heart be humble and receptive to
one another and to the things of God, not to the world.

Even before he made the world, God
loved us and chose us in Christ to be
holy and without fault in his eyes.

—EPHESIANS 1:4 NLT

*T*he simplest definition of *holy* is "being like God." That may involve a few or several of the practices I mentioned above, but none of them is the essence of holiness. If we want to be holy, we will pattern our lives after God as closely as possible. And just how do we do that? We have a perfect model: Jesus was *Emmanuel*—God with us. In the Gospels we can look at him at any time, whatever he is doing, and see exactly what God is like. In Jesus we see holiness in its purest form.

What do we see when we look at Jesus? How did he demonstrate holiness? Maybe the best answer is the one he gave to John the Baptist when John sent a message from his prison cell, questioning whether Jesus was the One they had been expecting God to send. To confirm that he was God's Holy One, Jesus did not send back the answer we might expect: "Tell John that I pray five times a day, fast three times a week, never eat without going through ritual purification, never miss a synagogue meeting, burn the midnight oil studying the holy scrolls, avoid everything unclean, and wouldn't touch a drop of wine even with gloves on." Instead, he responded, "Go back to John and tell him what you have heard and seen—the blind see, the lame walk, the lepers are cured, the deaf hear, the dead are raised to life, and the Good News is being preached to the poor" (Matt. 11:4–5 NLT).

Here Jesus shows us clearly that being holy does not mean wearing a suit and taking a Bible to church. It doesn't mean praying long, eloquent prayers; fasting like a weight-watcher; saying "praise the Lord" a lot; or holding up your hands in church. It means getting those hands involved in God's work. Getting them dirty. Being holy means feeding the hungry, seeing to the needs of the sick, helping people in trouble, and comforting them in grief. It means letting your hands be instruments of God's love. It means opening your life to God's Holy Spirit and allowing him to use you to bless others.

One of the best examples of holiness is Mother Teresa. She wasn't holy because she dressed in a starchy black nun's habit and lived a cloistered life of prayer and meditation. She was holy because she dedicated her life to ministering through hands-on, physical contact to the most shunned, ostracized, and repugnant people on earth—the lepers in the filth of Calcutta's slums.

I have seen similar examples of holiness firsthand. I was in Haiti in the aftermath of the January 2010 earthquake, and I'll never forget seeing teams of Samaritan's Purse volunteers meeting the needs of the devastated and demoralized around them out of the fullness of Christ's love within them. Or meeting the Haitian pastor who showed me his house that had crumbled under a five-story school building, killing his wife, baby, mother, and mother-in-law. Amid his unbearable grief was a deep commitment to reflect the reality of God's goodness in the chaos around him. I was so overtaken by the generosity I observed in those serving around me that I was inspired to lend a hand where I could, serving at feeding stations and providing moments of distraction for kids by playing with and praying for them. Even in the epicenter of tragedy, hope was contagious.

These dedicated Christians blessed others deeply. And they did it at considerable sacrifice to themselves. They did not get paid for their work. Some may have been supported by churches or donations, but many had no financial support and even paid their own travel expenses. Some of them lost salaries or shut down their own businesses for a time in order to bless others. Some were injured or came down with diseases in the course of their service.

BOTH JESUS AND MOTHER TERESA ARE CITED AS GREAT EXAMPLES OF PERSONAL HOLINESS. DO YOU KNOW ANYONE IN YOUR OWN LIFE WHO PROVIDES SUCH AN EXAMPLE? WHAT SETS HIM OR HER APART FROM OTHER PEOPLE? HOW CAN YOU BEGIN TO EMULATE THAT PERSON IN YOUR OWN CHRISTIAN WALK?

BEING HOLY AND HELPING OTHERS

*I*t's no coincidence that in my prayer of blessing I connect holiness with having hands that are "tender and helping, blessing those in need." The Bible shows us in many places that God connects holiness—being like him—with the way we care for others and meet their needs. Christ's answer to John quoted a few pages back is one example. Another is in John the apostle's letter, where he wrote, "For anyone who does not love his brother, whom he has seen, cannot love God, whom he has not seen. And he has given us this command: Whoever loves God must also love his brother" (1 John 4:20–21).

It's significant that when Jesus spoke to his disciples of final judgment, the criteria he used to separate the saved people from the lost was whether they had fed the hungry and thirsty, given shelter and clothes to the needy, looked after the sick, and comforted those in trouble with the authorities (Matt. 25:31–46). The people who did these unselfish deeds for others were the ones who were holy, the ones who were most like God.

I'm not trying to weigh you down with some sort of works-based theology here. If there's one thing I know, it's that there's nothing we can do to justify ourselves in the presence of a holy God. The apostle Paul makes that clear in his letter to the church in Ephesus: "For by grace you have been saved through faith. And this is not your own doing; it is the gift of God, not a result of works, so that no one may boast" (Eph. 2:8–9 ESV). But there is an undeniable relationship between faith and good works. One will lead to another. A vibrant and healthy faith will produce good works as surely as an apple tree will produce apples. They just go together. James puts it this way: "For as the body apart from the spirit is dead, so also faith apart from works is dead" (James 2:26 ESV).

Why does God put so much stress on our love for him being expressed through service to others? I think the answer is pretty simple. As the apostle John tells us, God is love (1 John 4:16). That's what he's about. God created us out of love, and he loves us in many ways—as an artist loves his painting, as a musician loves his song, as a father loves his child, and in a vivid image used over and over in the Bible, as a lover loves his beloved. Love is what God is all about.

When our first parents rejected God in Eden, he was heartbroken. But he honored their choice and stepped out of their lives, grieving at the separation and the pain and suffering their choice would bring to their race. In spite of this rejection of his love, God sent his Son to show his love, not only in the great sacrifice to atone for our sins but also to demonstrate his love hands-on by serving and ministering to the hurts and needs of those he encountered while he was here.

After Jesus returned to heaven to prepare for our coming, he gave us the high honor of being his body on earth. We are to be channels through which God's love flows to others. We allow him to use our hands and our hearts to provide the blessings he wants to give to those who hurt and grieve. That's what being like God means. That's being holy.

WHY IS HOLINESS IMPORTANT? WHAT IS ITS PURPOSE?

*T*ake some time to search your soul and see if you don't long to have the kind of character that will joyfully take the risk of investing what God has given to you. This is the kind of holiness that will cause God to smile at you and say, "Well done, good and faithful servant."

That's what I long to hear. That is why when I pray my prayer of blessing, I am praying for myself as well as others. I want to hear those dear words from Jesus. And I know I will never hear them if I take the safe and easy route of no risk. If I avoid the contamination of the slum or the sickbed, the distressed cry of the homeless, the hungry, or the devastated; if I ignore the pain and despair of my neighbor, I may lead an easier, safer, and less harried life, but I will miss out on enormous blessings that God longs to give me. One of the best lessons I've learned is that the act of blessing others boomerangs back to the blesser. Blessing others becomes its own blessing.

I want evil cleaned out of my life and replaced with true holiness so that I will become a vessel through which God's blessings can pour freely to those around me. I want to be an example to them. An example of one who is not caught in the downward drift of culture. One who forces selfishness out of his life by replacing it with God's love and service to others. One who changes his focus from inward to outward. One who is devoted to being holy as God is holy.

Holiness consists of doing the
will of God with a smile.

—MOTHER TERESA

FOR REFLECTION AND ACTION

WHAT ROADBLOCKS STAND IN THE WAY OF YOUR PATH
TO PERSONAL HOLINESS? HOW CAN YOU BEGIN TO
CLEAR THE WAY?

....

....

....

....

....

....

....

....

....

....

....

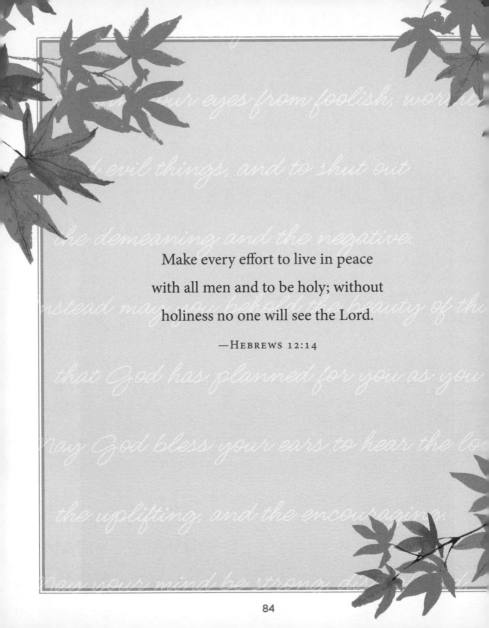

Make every effort to live in peace
with all men and to be holy; without
holiness no one will see the Lord.

—HEBREWS 12:14

CHAPTER 5

PRAYING FOR . . . BACKYARD BLESSINGS

God's grace be upon your home, that it may be a sanctuary of rest and renewal, a haven of peace where sounds of joy and laughter grace its walls, where love and unconditional acceptance of one another is the constant rule.

"As for me and my family, we

will serve the LORD."

—JOSHUA 24:15 NLT

Born as we are into a fallen race of sinners, we all tend to be selfish. We want things our way. We want what we want when we want it. Good parents do their best to train and discipline that selfishness out of us, and good teachers and pastors reinforce the lesson. But that self-centered tendency is deep-rooted, and it almost always requires hand-to-hand combat in the arena of life where the wants of self are pitted against the needs of others. Marriage and family provides this arena. Family is the perfect challenge to selfishness. Living in a family demands that I be sensitive to the needs of others. It demands my time. It intrudes on my wants. It tramples my ego. It virtually obliterates the concept of leisure. What a blessing!

No, I'm not being facetious; these duties are truly blessings. Without such duties, we would become utterly self-centered, egotistical, and narcissistic—all of which are deadly because focus on self alienates us from God. Facing up to our duties beats down selfishness and forms godly character by challenging the supremacy of self.

Let me be quick to say that marriage and family are not the only means of beating down the curse of selfishness. Many single people and childless couples are truly godly in character, compassionate, loving, and unselfish in all their doings. But I think marriage and family provide a rewarding means of dealing with selfishness because the glue that holds us to it when we'd rather bail out is love.

Had love not held us together, either my wife, Debbie, or I could've bailed out of the marriage or abandoned our family when the demands on self became too great. But we found—as all committed couples do—that if you hang in there, dedicate yourself to your family's welfare, and stick to it when you'd rather hit the road, having a family is one of the most character-forming experiences of all.

And the most rewarding.

IF YOU WERE TO MAKE UP A SLOGAN THAT DESCRIBES YOUR FAMILY, WHAT WOULD IT BE? WHAT WOULD YOU LIKE IT TO BE? HOW COULD YOU RECONCILE THE TWO?

*H*iding within all the pain and frustration that comes with family are some of the most enormous blessings God ever gives. Out of family emerges more joy than anyone deserves.

Last year as my family gathered around our dining room table on Father's Day, I paused a moment and just listened to the love. It was expressed in amiable conversation, jokes, and laughter. And I thought, *What I have here is a far better blessing than all the Grammy Awards I could ever win.* And I really meant it. I am doubly blessed that all my children and grandchildren live nearby. We share meals as often as three times a week.

I am triply blessed in that I live in a family that truly loves being together. My daughters Anna and Emily would admit, without hesitation, that they are the best of friends. How crazy is that!

I know of many families who are not together. For some, it's because of distance. For others it's by choice. I know families in which every get-together involves sadness, conflict, and heartbreak. When family relationships go sour, something vital is stolen from life. When things at home are not good, nothing seems good.

My point in all this is to say that dealing effectively with adversity is what makes family love and togetherness possible. If parents are not willing to face the adversity of sacrifice that comes with growing a marriage and raising a family, they cannot expect to reap the blessing of joy that only family can bring. Parents who try to escape the adversity by not making those sacrifices tend to end up with families that reflect the same kind of selfishness. When each is out to protect himself or herself from sacrifice, family members tend to find themselves at constant odds with other members whose very proximity and varying needs and wants intrude on their own.

After twenty-nine years of marriage and family, I tell you this with all sincerity: if it came down to a choice between family and music, believe me, I would choose family in a heartbeat. Because family is what makes my heart beat.

THE BIGGEST OBSTACLE TO BLESSINGS

*O*ne thing that really breaks my heart—and it's one of the reasons I wanted to write this book—is that everywhere I go I find so many people for whom marriage is far from being a source of joy. In fact, it is their main source of pain, sadness, and disillusionment. I hear of people living in misery because of loveless or abusive marriages. I hear of unfaithfulness, alcoholism, addiction, neglect, and emotional bullying. More often I hear of separations, abandonment, divorce, custody battles, alimony, and child-support neglect. I hear of single parents struggling desperately to keep things together. In almost every case there is anger, bitterness, disillusionment, or despair. Tell these people that marriage is a source of joy and they'll laugh in your face.

I know it's a hard thing to say, but I must say it: in almost every instance of a miserable or broken marriage, the root cause is selfishness. Don't get me wrong; I'm not judging or accusing. But I've seen situations where both parties were so ingrained in their own sense of entitlement that it made compromise nearly impossible. I've also seen this play out in a more one-sided fashion, as individuals in marriages become so preoccupied with their own needs that they completely alienate their spouse. It seems a bit unfair in today's world to pin the blame for self-centeredness solely on the individual when it seems that society as a whole has bent over backward to push us into self-assertiveness, self-actualization, self-esteem, self-determination, self-reliance, self-this and self-that. The total emphasis is on independence, rights, and expectations.

Self-sacrifice gets no press these days. In fact, we are encouraged against becoming "doormats," implying that sacrifice and giving will mean the loss of selfhood and personal happiness. That's why many couples marrying today have lawyers write up prenuptial contracts outlining marital expectations and property distribution, should divorce occur. When couples enter marriage with such demands, they miss out on the blessings that can come only from sacrificial love. They become open only to the getting and closed off from the giving. The bottled-up selfishness festers into discontent, which usually ruptures and destroys the marriage. With today's pervasive emphasis on meeting the demands of self, it's little mystery why the American divorce rate hovers at 50 percent.

In such a toxic environment, it's perfectly natural to think, *But if I follow the path of sacrifice and give up the things I've wanted and dreamed of for my life, how can I be happy?* Good question. On the surface it doesn't seem to make sense. It's one of those things we won't know until we try it. It's called stepping out in faith. Jesus himself assured us that giving up our lives is the only way to have life. "If you cling to your life, you will lose it; but if you give up your life for me, you will find it" (Matt. 10:39 NLT).

The more you think about that topsy-turvy statement, the more you can see the sense of it. The big emphasis today is on enjoying ourselves. But as someone once said, "Sooner or later we find that there is nothing left in the self to enjoy."

When unopened to others, the self is a closed prison. Locked inside that prison, we become dependent on our own resources for happiness, fulfillment, and meaning. But our own resources are limited. Once we fill ourselves by satisfying our wants, that hoard of gratification becomes our total supply of resources for enjoyment. And gratification of selfish desires always wears thin and becomes tiresome.

HOW WOULD AN ATTITUDE OF SERVANTHOOD DISPLAYED BY BOTH YOU AND YOUR FAMILY MEMBERS CHANGE THE DYNAMICS OF YOUR FAMILY? HOW COULD YOU PROMOTE SUCH A CHANGE IN ATTITUDE?

It's only when we open ourselves outward in giving to others that our own meager resources can be replaced with the fresh ones God wants to pour in. We are created for connection, for relationships. Relationships are maintained by a continual mutual flow of giving to one another. That interplay of love washes out the canker of selfishness and produces blessings.

BLESSING YOUR FAMILY

*A*s a father, there's one thing I can do to pass along the backyard blessings of marriage and family. I can put every ounce of ability and energy I have into instilling into my children these principles of happiness in relationships. With all my heart I want my own children to find the same kind of joy in family that I have found. How do I do that?

This is not easy in a world where the culture seems to be conspiring against you. Epidemic marriage failure is driving today's young people to live together instead of marrying. This, in turn, has driven the illegitimate birthrate almost to 50 percent. These children grow up without models for family happiness, often without any sort of Christlike example.

Even those raised by Christian parents and regularly taken to church are leaving the church in droves. Without principles to guide them, they are vulnerable to the pitfalls of the entertainment culture, which inevitably exposes them to sensuality and perversion. The proliferation of iPods, social websites, and smart phones often closes them off into a world of electronic communication that can effectively separate them from parental influence. Subverted by godless worldviews in public schools and unbelieving professors in college, they are easily seduced into the godless thinking of today.

To counter this formidable onslaught against the family, parents must be intentional, vigilant, and committed. It must start early. In those first years when parents have their kids' attention and respect, the groundwork must be laid for what is right and wrong, allowable and not. They must show their love by being willing to discipline. It's not always easy, but parents must stick to their guns. Deb and I have been blessed with five *great* kids. But even the most well-behaved child needs to develop a strong sense of right and wrong. This means there are certain things other kids do that your kids can't. Places other kids go that yours can't.

All this must be balanced with what they can do. Give them your time. Children spell love, T-I-M-E. This doesn't mean just "quality time." That's a myth. The *quantity* of time is really more important, even if you're not doing anything exciting or meaningful while you're together. It's not as hard as we think. Take them with you on your errands. Have fun with them while working together. Plan excursions. Movies, concerts, and plays are okay, but also expose them to the great outdoors. Go hiking. Play baseball. Take them fishing. Spread a quilt on the grass on a summer night and spend an hour or so gazing at the backyard blessing of a sky full of stars.

Early on, show them the nature of God through his creation. Teach them to love it. Lead them to understand that the best things in life are free. You can't buy more spectacular sights than great mountains, multicolored sunsets, billowing clouds, migrating bird formations, a field of flowers accented with flitting butterflies. If these things seem trite to kids today (and to adults as well), it's because we've allowed the overstimulation of popular culture to dull our sensitivity to natural, everyday wonders that are truly spectacular.

In our culture of inverted values, God's creation is to most people a place to escape to for a few days before coming back to the *real* world where the true action is. That outlook brings our task with our families into focus. We must make God's world real to them. We must show them that what comes from him is the true reality. I'm not talking just about nature; I'm speaking of moral values, integrity, selfless love, respect for others, sacrificial living, and commitment to God and his truth. That's the family blessing you want to pass on to your children.

The bottom line is this: we must educate our kids in addition to what the schools and churches do. Make your love for them and for God visible and real. Don't just teach it; live it before them in a way that they absorb it. Don't just tell your children; *show* them what living holy is like.

Families that learn to do this successfully will find the blessing of God's grace upon their home. It will be a sanctuary of rest and renewal, a haven of peace where sounds of joy and laughter grace its walls, where love and unconditional acceptance of one another is the rule.

That is the blessing I pray for you and your family.

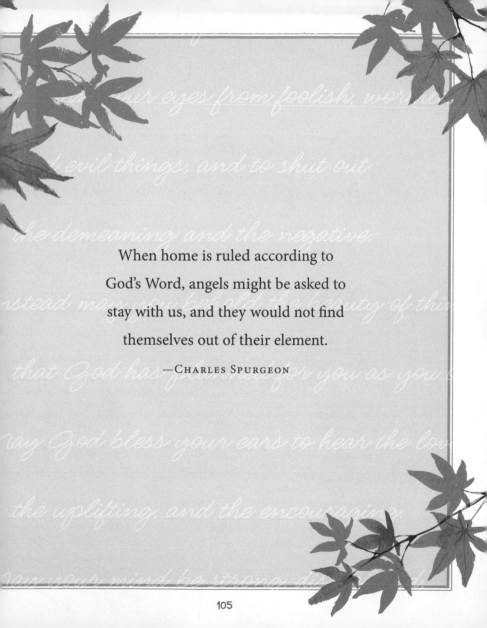

When home is ruled according to God's Word, angels might be asked to stay with us, and they would not find themselves out of their element.

—Charles Spurgeon

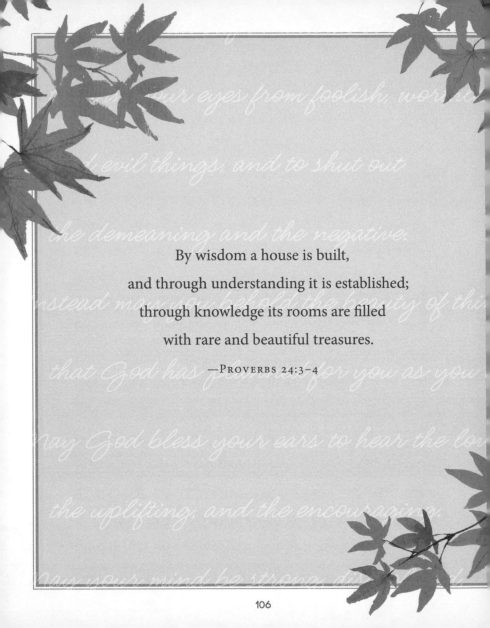

By wisdom a house is built,

and through understanding it is established;

through knowledge its rooms are filled

with rare and beautiful treasures.

—Proverbs 24:3–4

FOR REFLECTION AND ACTION

WHAT IS ONE PRACTICAL WAY YOU CAN IMPROVE THE
WAY YOU TREAT EACH MEMBER OF YOUR FAMILY THIS
WEEK? HOW CAN YOU LET EACH FAMILY MEMBER KNOW
WHAT A BLESSING THEY ARE?

CHAPTER 6

PRAYING FOR . . .
SPIRITUAL VICTORY

May God give you the spiritual strength to overcome the
evil one and avoid temptation. May God's grace be upon
you to fulfill your dreams and visions. May goodness
and mercy follow you all the days of your long life.

But thanks be to God! He gives us the
victory through our Lord Jesus Christ.

—1 CORINTHIANS 15:57

I firmly believe in the power of words to bless people. As I've said, it's not because of any magic in the words themselves. It's because of their power in conveying your care and love.

But I wouldn't be telling you the whole truth if I left you with the impression that words alone are always adequate. There is a time for words, and there is a time for action. As James tells us:

> Suppose you see a brother or sister who has no food or clothing, and you say, "Good-bye and have a good day; stay warm and eat well"—but then you don't give that person any food or clothing. What good does that do?
>
> (James 2:15–16 NLT)

The apostle Paul told us to make it a habit to be encouragers (1 Thess. 5:11). This is a way of blessing people we encounter, even when we know nothing about them or their needs. James, on the other hand, is saying, "Don't resort to mere words of encouragement when you encounter people facing a visible need for hands-on help." He's warning us against being all talk when it's obvious that action is needed.

Blessing with words should be a policy that we follow in all our dealings with people in general. Blessing with actions applies specifically to those tangible needs that God places in front of us.

We've all had experiences when we've seen a need and felt our hearts leap out of our chests—as if God himself were in us saying, "Do it for my sake." It could be an elderly neighbor across the street in need of help with the lawn, or a child on the other side of the globe who needs sponsorship through an organization like Compassion International. When we encounter a real need that we can meet personally, that's when, as James points out, words alone are not enough.

Jesus taught that the needs of our neighbor are always our responsibility. "And who is my neighbor?" the Pharisees asked him. Jesus answered with the parable of the Good Samaritan, which shows that our neighbor is any person we come across who has a need that we have the power to meet (Luke 10:27–37). That means your family all the time. It means your friends, coworkers, and fellow believers as you see needs arise in their lives. More than that, as Jesus' parable shows, your neighbor can be anyone you encounter who has a need that you can meet. You have the power to bless these people both in word and in deed by loaning God your hands to meet their need.

About a year ago, I was running an errand on a Sunday afternoon. Along the way I saw a middle-aged man sitting at the side of the road. His clothes were dirty, and the expression on his face gave away the heaviness that he carried in his heart. He was holding a sign asking for food. I was compelled to help, so I pulled into the nearest fast-food place and ordered something. His eyes lifted as I pulled up and got out of the car, as if he was surprised that I was there. I gave him the food that I had ordered and sat down to talk with him for a while. He shared that he had spent the morning sitting near the entrance to a church nearby. His words were saturated with bitterness as he explained that none of the people who left the entrance of the church that morning had given him a second glance. My heart ached, and I offered an apology.

This man didn't know who I was, nor did I know who he was. And I'm quite sure that the fast food that I offered him wasn't going to solve all of his problems. But the simple fact that someone showed him compassion in the form of food and a kind word moved him. He hadn't experienced kindness from anyone for quite a while. He ate his food and expressed his thanks as I went on my way.

DESIRING A BLESSING

*W*e've spent most of this book talking about how Christ followers should focus not on themselves but on blessing others. And we've shown how blessing others inevitably results in blessings for ourselves. God blesses us in proportion to how we open our hands to receive his blessing, and how open our hands remain in passing on his blessings to those who need them.

I want to assure you that it's not wrong for you to desire a blessing for yourself. Remember Jacob? He went so far as to wrestle with God for a personal blessing. And he got it (Gen. 32:24–30).

God wants to bless you as much as you want to be blessed. Let's face it: we all need blessing. It's part of our lot in this fallen world to have hurts and needs. And it's part of God's intention for us to have dreams and aspirations that we desire to have fulfilled. We naturally want God's blessings to see us through our hurts and to fulfill those dreams.

WHAT DOES THE STATEMENT, "GOD WANTS TO BLESS YOU AS MUCH AS YOU WANT TO BE BLESSED," MEAN TO YOU? DOES IT RUN COUNTER TO YOUR IDEA OF GOD'S CHARACTER? WHY OR WHY NOT? HOW DOES YOUR CONCEPT OF GOD AFFECT THE BLESSINGS THAT YOU RECEIVE ON A DAILY BASIS?

$\mathcal{I}$ pray that God will bless you by fulfilling your dreams. At the same time, I pray that your dreams will rise higher than career success or wealth or pleasure. I hope you will open yourself to God's blessing by dreaming the dream God has for you. He is your Maker, and he made you as a unique being with attributes and abilities that make you different from any other person ever created. He made you this way because he has a function for you to fulfill that you can do better than any other person on earth. He wants to bless you by putting you in a place where you can fulfill it.

This means that when we pray for God's blessing, we are praying for God to put us where he intended for us to be, doing what he intended for us to do. If we work against God's intention, we will be working against the blessing he wants to give. If a fish were to dream of soaring among the clouds like an eagle, I'm pretty sure God would not bless that dream. God didn't equip a fish to fly. Our dreams must match God's purpose for our lives.

Sometimes God's purpose is not immediately clear to us. Many people live in frustration because they cannot find the place where they seem to fit. How do we find that place? Sometimes it shows up clearly in our talents and our desires. The first time I sat at a piano, something clicked in my soul, and I knew what I was meant to do. But for many others, the path is foggy and obscure. And the reasons can vary. I believe that many unintentionally bury God's intent for them under ambitions they pick up from the surrounding culture. In a wealth-and-success-oriented society, it's easy for one's ambitions to follow the popular concept of success and miss out on the higher and happier life God wants to give you.

If the path to that higher and happier life is not clear, you can take positive steps toward finding it. You can pray for guidance and then tune your spirit to hear the answer by spending time in God's Word and quiet meditation. You can seek the counsel of trusted Christian mentors. Committed friends who know you and have your wellbeing at heart can often see things about you that are not clear to yourself.

When you ask for the blessing of having your dreams fulfilled, it's important that you get on the same page with God. If he gave you fins, you face only frustration if you pursue a dream that requires wings. A person who stands four foot eleven should not dream of playing in the NBA. Nor should a person who stands six foot six dream of being a racehorse jockey. To be truly blessed, you must set your sights on what God has equipped you to be.

"But," you may say, "I've always wanted to be a doctor. What if God wants me to be an accountant? I hate working with figures. Doesn't God want me to be joyful in my Christian life? How can I be joyful doing something I hate?"

Well, I don't think God will ask you to do something you truly hate. It's likely he will put into your heart a desire to do what he intends for you. Sometimes that desire may be buried, and you may need to dig it out from under all the other desires you've heaped on top of it. That's where prayer and counsel come into play.

I think we can safely say that you'll never find joy in making yourself into something God didn't intend. You will find joy only in being all he wants you to be. The apostle Paul gives us the key in Romans 8:28: "And we know that God causes everything to work together for the good of those who love God *and are called according to his purpose for them*"(NLT; emphasis added). God has a purpose for you, and he calls you to it. If you don't hear that call, the way to receive the blessing it promises is to clear from your mind the clutter of your own desires. Then pray, seek counsel, and listen until God's will becomes clear.

WHAT DREAMS HAS GOD GIVEN YOU THAT HAVE BEEN FULFILLED? WHAT DREAMS HAS GOD PLANTED IN YOUR HEART THAT ARE STILL WAITING TO BE FULFILLED? HOW CAN YOU SUBMIT ALL OF YOUR DREAMS TO THE ONE WHO WANTS TO FULFILL THEM? (BE AS PRACTICAL AS YOU CAN.)

I do not presume to know God's purpose for your life. You may be given talents that call you to the ministry or to some profession or trade. But wherever God puts you, I am sure of this: He wants to bless you. And he wants you to bless others through his gifts to you. That is the only way your dreams and visions can be fulfilled.

Submit to God's will for you, and you can be sure that goodness and mercy will follow you all the days of your life, and you will dwell in the house of the Lord forever.

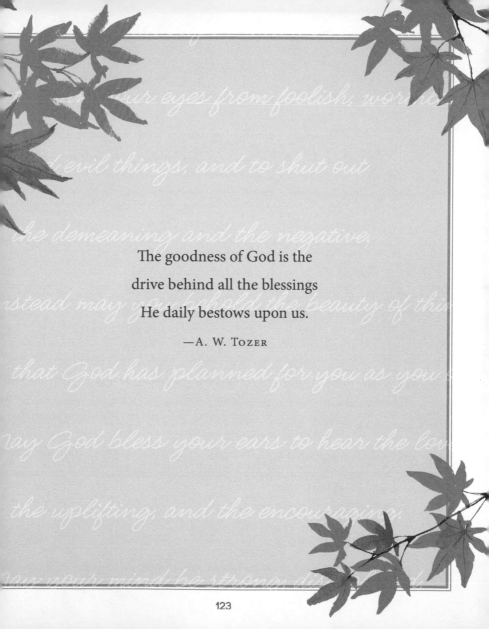

The goodness of God is the
drive behind all the blessings
He daily bestows upon us.

—A. W. TOZER

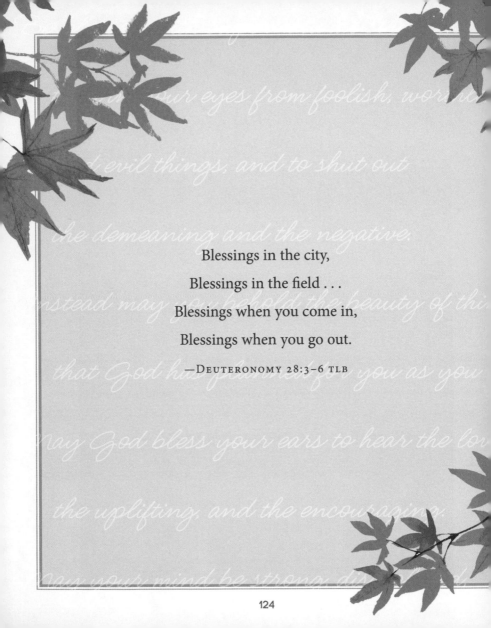

Blessings in the city,

Blessings in the field . . .

Blessings when you come in,

Blessings when you go out.

—Deuteronomy 28:3–6 TLB

FOR REFLECTION AND ACTION

HOW IS YOUR LIFE AN EXAMPLE OF THE PHRASE "BLESSED TO BE A BLESSING"? IN WHAT SPECIFIC WAYS CAN YOU USE THE BLESSINGS YOU CURRENTLY ENJOY TO BLESS OTHER PEOPLE IN TURN?

....

....

....

....

....

....

....

....

....

....

The LORD bless you, and keep you; the
LORD make His face shine on you, and
be gracious to you; the LORD lift up His
countenance on you, and give you peace.

—NUMBERS 6:24–26 NASB

ABOUT THE AUTHOR

*I*n addition to winning several Grammy and Dove awards, Michael W. Smith has recorded more than twenty-five albums and had numerous hit radio songs in the Christian and general markets. He is also involved in mission work at home and around the world, and is the founder of Rocketown, an outreach to teenagers in a 38,000-square-foot facility in downtown Nashville, Tennessee. He has written several best-selling books, including *Old Enough to Know* and *Friends Are Friends Forever*. He and his wife, Debbie, have five children and live in Nashville.